HOW TO

PLAY
BASKETBALL
THE FUN
WAY

 Introduction and Thank You

This is a book of real-life events. Names, places and events are from the author's perspective. © 2020 by Jenarie Middleton
Basketball (Real-Time Photos) by: Stephron Photography
Cover Imaged Arranged by: Jenarie Middleton
Edited by: Jenarie Middleton
Self Published Through BookBaby
ISBN 9781098320409 (paperback)
Printed in The United States of America

I started my journey in writing this book in my junior year of high school in 2002. Furthermore, I proceed to give a very brief shout out to those who made it possible for me to write this book. I would like to first thank The Most High for his grace, love and discipline over my life. I would like to thank my parents, Aaron and Stephanie Teel. My Grandparents and Great Grandparents, Leran/Mary, Johnny/Mildred and James/Sarah. My Uncle Randy/Auntie Myra. Thank you to my siblings and cousins, Justin, Shala/Michael Armstrong, Tamar, Kendra and Doran and also my God Mother and Sisters, Annette, Lynette, Maranda and Seprina. I send a huge thank you to my five children and Husband, Bernard. They are the ones who kept me grounded and motivated me to implement love in my life no matter what. I love you all very dearly. Thank you to Life Coach, D Nicole Williams and Author, Liltera Williams. With your acquired knowledge; I was able to "Live My Dream," and "Change My Posture."

 About The Author

There was a time when I only watched Basketball on TV. I never thought I would one day love playing it so much. My friends in Middle School were good and I tried out for the girl's team and made it on the squad. Every chance I had, I practiced and learned from watching NBA Players like: Allen Iverson and Kobe Bryant. My Dad and Uncle taught me everything about the basic skills I needed in order to get better. I am very thankful for their tenacity with helping me succeed. Please enjoy this book as we made it easy for you to follow, while you learn how to play basketball the fun way. -Jenarie Middleton

"Give honor to THE MOST HIGH. Give him all the praise in all that you say and do. He is the ultimate light in your life. Whatever you gain is from his glory and his glory alone." -Jenarie Middleton

Visit Jenarie's Website: www.4Jenarie.wordpress.com

Rest In Love Uncle Alex

Preface

Children listen to your elders. Follow your parent's instructions. Seek good things. Deter away from the nonsense and ruckus. Avoid mistreating your peers. Everyone who surrounds you may not be good for you. There's a saying, "You reap what you sow." Seek wisdom and knowledge and understanding. Let the truth be your peacemaker. Don't be the person always proving yourself right in the midst of cowards. Be straightforward in your approach. Don't cause trouble and then walk away. Leave your footsteps behind so others can follow them. Let your foot lead with good intentions and not with evil. Don't lean on your own understanding. As high as you can soar, you can also plummet hard to the ground. Show love to people and you will get love back. Be kind, but be diligent also. Don't allow your naivety to overcome your judgment. Keep focus and be aware. ~Jenarie

Lastly, A huge thank you goes to my mother. When I wanted to quit and give up. She wouldn't allow me to. As I get closer to the age of 40, she still won't allow me to fall short of my negative thoughts. She reels me back in with her long fishing pole. Grabbing me tight, holding me as I cry. Telling me that I am loved and able. I love my mother forever.

When I was in college when I felt weak, my mother left me with handwritten notes. She gifted me with some things during those tough movements that I still have today. I promised that I'd stay focused and finish school and I did. I thank my Dad as well.

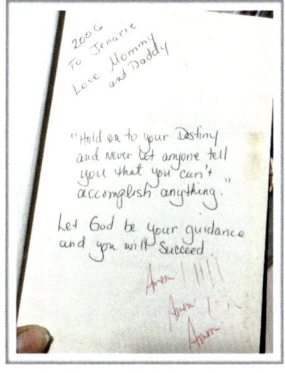

He didn't show the nurturing love my mother had, but he gave stability. He wasn't always present because of his work schedule, but he gave me the tools I needed to start. Daddy was the one who told me to write this book. Everything that I went through lead to what I accomplished thus far. He always told me, "I will show you what to do, but it's up to you to finish on your own." And I did just that! For the last 13 years, I've become a mother to five amazingly/talented children and a wife to my wonderful husband. They helped me become the woman I am today.

Table of Contents

1. 🏀
HOW TO DRIBBLE THE BALL THE FUN WAY

STEP 1:

- ✓ The Best way to Dribble is to pat the ball with your fingertips.

STEP 2:

- ✓ Sit in a chair with your back straight and knees bent.

STEP 3:

- ✓ Pat the ball with your fingertips as fast as you can. If you mess up, it's okay just keep going.

- ✓ Practice guarding the ball with your other arm by holding it up as if you were looking down at your watch to see what time it is. This helps protect the ball from another player when they are trying to take the ball away from you during a game.

- ✓ Practice using your opposite hand as well. Do this for 5 minutes on each hand.

Soon you'll be able to stand up from your chair and dribble. Please practice patting the ball with your left and right hand all the time.

Do these steps every day as often as possible. The more you work to get better, the better you will become.

2. 🏀
HOW TO HOLD THE BASKETBALL THE FUN WAY (TRIPLE THREAT POSITION)

Step 1:

✓ The fun way of holding the basketball is to grab it with both of your hands. Put the hand you shoot with on top of the ball. Then place your other hand on the side of the ball to help guide your shot or pass. Holding the ball like this is also called, *"The Triple Threat Position."* The triple threat position allows a player to pass the ball, shoot the ball or dribble the ball when needed. You can go left, right or forward in this position.

Step 2:

✓ Make sure to practice slap/patting the ball with both hands without your palms touching the ball. Doing this drill will strengthen your hands and arms. When you hold the ball in the triple threat position with pride and strength, no one can take the ball away from you. The objective is to protect the ball in your possession. Avoiding fewer unforced turnovers and to secure the ball in order to score as many points as possible to win the game.

Step 3:

✓ In the triple threat position, you can go either direction. Keep the ball on the side of your body and move it quickly from side to side. Never place the ball in front of you; unless you are ready to shoot or pass the ball to your teammate.

✓ While in triple threat position, attack the basket head-on in a straight line. Be aggressive in your approach toward the basket. Think about the letter V. With you being in front of your opponent, you must look at your position on the court, see the basket and attack the basket. Dribble with purpose straight ahead (not allowing your opponent to take you too far to the left or right). Attack the basket

straight and decide whether you will use **The Pull-Up Jumper**, finish with a **Lay Up** to the basket or **Passing** the ball to your teammate for an open shot. Attacking the basket creates opportunities for yourself to become a magnet. The defense will adjust and will defend their basket by shifting their concentration towards you. This sometimes may cause one of your teammates to be open. In a case like this, you can pass the ball to your open teammate for an assist. Always observe the court, head on a swivel.

You may drop the ball a few times; you may even jam your thumb, but it's okay, just keep on going! Never give up!

Triple Threat Dribble To The Left

Don't Be Afraid of Contact

Triple Threat Dribble To The Right

Triple Threat Dribble To The Left Front View

Head Up

Observe The Court

Attack The Basket

3. 🏀
HOW TO PASS THE BASKETBALL THE FUN WAY

Step 1:

✓ When you pass the Basketball, the palm of your hand(s) should not touch the ball. This is the same technique from Chapter 2; **Holding the Ball the Fun Way.** Your ball control will enhance. Practice passing the basketball by yourself or with a partner so that your passing skills may improve. Find a wall near the basketball court or in the basketball gym to use. If you are not able to go to a court, ask your parents or siblings to practice with you at home.

Step 2:

✓ Set a target on the wall. Aim your pass with the ball at that spot. Your goal is to hit that spot continuously with accuracy. Use your right and left hand, passing at your target 25 times with each hand.

✓ If you have a partner, practice using both hands as well.

🏀 Two-Hand Chest Pass 🏀

Here are different ways of passing the basketball:

🏀 Two-Hand Bounce Pass 🏀

🏀 Overhead Pass 🏀

🏀 One Hand Baseball Pass (Right) 🏀

🏀 <u>One Hand Baseball Pass (Left)</u> 🏀

With time your ball control and the accuracy of your pass will improve. Then you can add other passing techniques like: **The Wrap Around Pass, The Lob Pass** and **The Baseball Pass.**

Fundamentals will carry your game a long way and will make a major difference in how you'll excel through each level of basketball you reach. Below are a few pictures of how you should throw the baseball pass with your left andright hand.

4. 🏀
HOW TO SHOOT THE BASKETBALL THE FUN WAY (JUMP SHOT/LAYUP)

Here's a little advice before reading the first step into shooting a basketball into the hoop. Don't think too hard when shooting the basketball. It can be tricky at times. Sooner or later you will get stronger to shoot on any basket, small or tall. Practice shooting with a toy ball into a laundry basket 🧺 with your siblings, your cousins or just by yourself. Make it fun……

Step 1:

- ✓ Hold the ball with your fingertips. Before letting your shot go (to shoot the ball), make sure you're holding it up like a ball on a mantel.

- ✓ There should be a space between the palm of your hand and the ball, which will rest on the top of your fingertips. This technique allows your ball to spin, soaring high and dropping low. It's called an arch to your shot. Just like the force of gravity, "Whatever goes up must come down." I'm sure you have learned about "Newton's Law," in school by now!

Step 2:

- ✓ You will do the same technique when doing a lay-up.

- ✓ A lay-up is a type of shot that is completed on a fast break

✓ Thrust your leg up toward your chest with a bent knee, finishing with one hand elevated toward the basket. Preferably aiming at the backboard right behind the basketball rim. Better known as the (Square) or (Box).

✓ If you are attempting a lay-up on the right side, your right leg and right arm should be elevated toward the basket. The same goes for the left side.

✓ If you're attempting a lay-up on the left side, your left leg and left arm should be elevated up toward the basket.

✓ Finish the lay-up with ease. Aiming your shot too hard at the backboard or rim will cause you to miss the basket. Better known as a Brick.

Chapter 4 (Bonus)

🏀 Lie on the floor at night and practice shooting the ball into the air. Shoot towards the ceiling, aiming high (the ball should not hit the ceiling). Remember to have your shooting hand placed at the top of the ball using your fingertips. Then use your other hand to guide the ball's direction.

🏀 Bend your arm at the elbow with the ball near your face while holding the ball with your guide hand.

🏀 Lift your arm and push it straight up. When you release the ball, let it go at the top of your fingertips and snap your wrist. This technique will give your shot a high arch creating more space for your shot to fall in the basket accurately.

🏀 My Uncle Randy used to tell me, "Jenarie, when you snap your wrist say this to yourself, How Ya Doin!" It was an easy way for me to always remember shooting the correct way by snapping my wrist!

 Set Shot 🏀

A set shot is when you shoot in place without taking a dribble

🏀 Shooting a set shot with a defender 🏀

🏀 <u>Shooting the ball off the dribble</u> 🏀

Shooting the ball off the dribble is normally taken during a transition play from a fast break or from the triple threat position driving the ball toward the basket by taking 2-4 dribbles. Also from the triple threat position, scope the defense and if your opponent hand is down and you're in range to shoot, then shoot your best shot. Always look up toward the basket. Never dribble the ball with your head down.

Shooting the Lay Up

When shooting a layup from the left side, bend your left leg and left arm. Shooting a layup from the right side, bend your right leg and right arm. Make sure your aim is at the top corner of the square.

🏀 Shooting the Lay Up (Left & Right) Side 🏀

🏀 Shooting From The Free Throw Line 🏀

Bend your knees and hold the ball from the shooting position. Raise arms up in front of your face (bending at the elbow). Then push your shooting arm straight up, shooting above the rim. Your, (How Ya Doin') snapping your wrist follow-through will help the ball fall into the basket.

5. 🏀
HOW TO PLAY DEFENSE THE FUN WAY

When you think of defense in basketball, what comes to mind? Do you know anything about playing defense? Well, as for me, playing defense was my favorite. It fueled me. Playing defense prepared me to score on the offensive end. Offense is when it's your team's opportunity to score. It's exciting when you can stop the other team and their players from scoring. You can take the ball away from them and you can deflect their passes. When I learned how to play in 1997, I was 12 years old. The first thing I learned was defense. I didn't know how to shoot or dribble the ball. My father taught me the importance of timing the ball.

Timing the ball is an art. If you can time the ball right, you can steal the ball away from other player(s) at any time. It's not too difficult. All you have to do is have fun. Here's what you should do.

Step 1:

- ✓ When the ball comes down from your opponent's hand, that's the time when the ball is away from their possession. That's your chance to swipe the ball away.

- ✓ Always make sure that when you swipe at the ball, that you swipe up with your palm open, hitting the ball upwards with your fingertips. Never swipe down or swipe from left to right. If you do swipe like that, the referee will most likely call a personal foul on you in that possession.

- ✓ Also, never I repeat never swipe at the ball from behind the other player. When I was a collegiate athlete I took an elbow to my face and eventually lost my two front teeth. If you go from behind them

✓ You can receive a foul or risk getting injured. A future Hall of Fame, retired NBA player (Dirk Nowitzki) of "The Dallas Mavericks," tried to swipe the ball away (downward) from player (Terry Porter). He attempted to deflect the ball and took an elbow to the face and lost his two front teeth, just like I did. However, he continued to play in that very game with missing teeth. Finishing the game against, "The San Antonio Spurs" that night with 30 points, 9 rebounds and 10 assists, beating the Spurs by 4 points (112-108).

Step 2:

WAIT............ I know what I just mentioned above in step 1 was pretty intense. So please don't feel unsure about playing basketball now. Basketball is a contact sport, but injuries like losing your teeth is very rare. It's safe to say that using a mouth guard to protect your teeth is great. Ask your parents to have one made for you so you can protect your beautiful smile!

Now here's Step 2:

✓ Watch the dribbler's hips. Their hips will tell you which direction they're going in. Never mind their feet, pay attention to the hips!

Step 3:

✓ Bend your knees and slide your feet from left to right. Back straight with arms spread out and wide, don't get too close.

✓ Make sure you are far away enough to stay in front of your opponent. If you get too close they can dribble past you very quickly.

Defensive Stance

 Defend the ball in a low stance. Keep your back straight and feet evenly spread apart

KEEP YOUR ARMS OUT AND WIDE

STAY IN FRONT & SLIDE YOUR FEET

6. 🏀
HOW TO REBOUND THE BALL THE FUN WAY

Have you ever had a balloon get stuck at the top of the ceiling at home? You would jump as high as you can to get it back down right? Well, in basketball rebounding is done the same way. However, you won't be the only one jumping to get the ball.

Step 1:

- ✓ The best way to getting the rebound is by positioning yourself in front of the person on the other team.

- ✓ Bend your knees low and feel the person behind you using your butt and arms. Then jump up for the ball in arms reach.

Step 2:

- ✓ Grab the basketball with two hands and pull it down close to your body. If you are tall you want to grab it and keep it high away from the shorter player(s) below you.

Don't be afraid. Pretend that the ball is the balloon that used to get stuck at the top of the ceiling at home. Grab it and never let it go. Well, until it's time to pass it to your teammate that is.

 Chapter 6 (Bonus)

There are terms that players and coaches use on the court to describe rebounding. When you're **fighting for position** to jump for the rebound you first **close out the shooter,** then you will **box your opponent out**. The other team will miss their shots, so be prepared to anticipate the shot not going in the basket.

The best position leading up to the rebound is to **front your man.** Knees bent and back straight. Thrust upward toward the ball, grabbing it with both hands.

 **Closeout the offensive shooter with one hand up and feet on guard**

 **They may Pump Fake so don't always fall for the shot attempt**

STAY LOW AND MOVE YOUR FEET

 To be ready to Defend the shot Attempt You must Close Out Your Opponent

 This prepares you to anticipate your opponent's next move

 Also, **Box Out** your opponent/shooter with your knees bent and back straight

STAND STRONG & HOLD YOUR GROUND

7. 🏀
HOW TO CONDITION YOUR BODY THE FUN WAY

Basketball is a tough sport. You have to run and jump a lot. You use your entire body to play. Staying in shape is a necessity. The younger you are the less you have to do to compete well. You have more energy and can withstand the many exercises and drills.

These are some fun ways to stay in shape and condition your body!

🏀 Stretching: Stretch for 20 minutes before you practice.

🏀 Push-Up Claps: Push-up and clap your partners hand 20 reps x 3 (or) by yourself. If you are alone push up and tap the basketball with one alternating hand in front of you.

🏀 Squat Bull Frog Jumps: Squat down low and jump straight up in the air reaching as far as possible. You can also squat down low and jump forward to five spots using exercising cones or chalk. Draw on the ground where your five spots will end. Do 5 reps jumping forward and turn around jogging back to the starting spot x 5.

🏀 Defensive Slides (Low Block -To- Low Block): (Do this alone or with a partner) If you do this drill with a partner, pass the ball to one another sliding your feet. Left to right and right to left from low block-to-low block for 30 seconds (or) 1-minute x 3. When alone, slide from j block to low block left to right and right to left for 30 seconds to 1-minute x 3.

Lateral Push-Up Hold: Extend your arms out in front of you in a push-up position (with your hands shaped like a diamond) and hold it for 30 seconds to 1 minute x 3. Make sure your hips are positioned evenly (center yourself). Your butt shouldn't be in the air, squeeze your glutes and hold in your stomach.

Dribbling Wall Sits: (Use one or two basketballs) If you use one basketball make sure you are using the correct form. Back straight against the wall, legs apart and arm-bar in front. (Just like the picture in chapter 1) Do this for 30 seconds to 1 minute x 3.

Jumping Jacks with Weights: Use (5lbs - 10lbs) 30 reps x 3

Long Lunges: Stand with legs (shoulders width apart) and lunge forward with your right foot first. Your left knee will bend almost touching the ground. Never rest your hands on your front forward knee. Keep your hands on your hips or behind your head for support instead. Do 5 reps on both legs (left and right) 5 times each x 3.

Push-Ups: Do 50-100 push-ups per day.

Run 1 Mile: Run one mile at least two times per week.

- Walk one time around the track before running your first lap. If you're not near a track, find a safe area to run. Run with a friend or run with your parents or guardians. Never run alone. Be cautious of your surroundings.

- Lap 1 and 2 pace yourself and jog.

- Lap 3 Run with medium speed.

- Lap 4 Flash Run with a medium pace on the first curve and straight away. Then sprint the last curve and straight away to the finish. Remember to breathe in your nose and out of your mouth.

STRETCH WITH A PURPOSE

TAKE DEEP BREATHS IN BETWEEN

This stretch relaxes the lower back.

 Chapter 7 Bonus

Believe it or not, wearing the right socks and undergarments can help with your training. Comfortable socks and foot soles can save you from injury to the lower half of your body. (See chapter 8)

- Change out your socks, undershirts, underwear and sports bras and tights often (Especially when playing in a tournament). You will play multiple games and it's best to stay fresh and prepared for the next game.

- Pack extra clothes in three's (3 pairs of socks, 3 pairs of tights and shorts, 3 pairs of tanks and bras, etc).

- Young ladies must have feminine hygiene products on hand as well, like wipes, deodorant, etc.

- Young men be prepared as well.

A few things you should always carry with you that are not pictured:
Deodorant, Hand Sanitizer, Hand Towel, Tooth Paste, Extra Shorts and Foot (Gel) Inserts. Feel free to add anything that you may need. Limit bringing personal items that are valuable to you unless it's your phone and identification card. Never leave your bag unattended and except when it's near your coaches or teammates while you are playing.

8. 🏀
PROTECTING YOUR BODY

Your body is very important so take care of it. Injuries and getting hurt happens and it is NOT fun. Here are some ways to avoid injury on and off the court and to keep a healthy body for years to come.

1. Eat green leafy vegetables like spinach, string beans, kale, romaine lettuce, asparagus, and cabbage.

2. Drink plenty of fluids like: water (with fruits veggies and lemons), cranberry juice, Pedialyte and homemade smoothies. The less sugar intake the better. Avoid beverages like; soda, Kool-Aid and high fructose juices.

3. Build your body with light weight training and cardio exercises like; yoga, pilates and calisthenics. Calisthenics are exercises consisting of using your own bodyweight like; push-ups, chin-ups, lunges, etc.

4. Receive **Pre/Post Massage** as much as possible. This will help to flush out the bad toxins in your body. Lactic Acid is bad waste stored in the muscle which causes leg cramps, limited range of motion (ROM) and bad flexibility. After workouts and practice, icing helps with inflamed and sore muscles. You will have to use this technique after practice or at night before going to bed. **R.I.C.E.** (**Rest** **Ice** **Compress** **Elevate**)

5. Use protective gear like; ankle braces, knee pads, shoulder and legs sleeves and a mouth guard. Wearing them prevents ankle sprains, ACL/Knee injuries and loss of front teeth. Wear crew styled (long thick) socks and high top shoes to support your ankles.

6. Protect yourself during the game. If you are shooting a layup near the basket or jumping for a rebound, and someone fouls you hard, be strong enough to take the hit. Curl your body up and fall to the ground. Avoid falling on your tale bone or head if possible. Be aware of your surroundings. Most basketball injuries come from within the paint (low post area).

7. Protect your feet/ankles, head/face and ribs. Basketball is a contact sport. If you play hard you might get bumped here or there on a few occasions. Create a guard up by holding your arms toward your sides with your elbows pointing down on **Man to Man** coverage on defense, (especially when boxing out the offensive player). Keep the basketball close to your body when attacking the basket on a layup in the paint as well. Defending the ball and your body on an offensive play is key when finishing your pull up short jumper or layup. Going up strong is great, but going up strong and smart is better.

Black Bean Veggie Burgers

Mixed veggies with sautéed Turkey Sausage

9. 🏀
LEARNING THE HISTORY AND UNDERSTANDING THE GAME OF BASKETBALL THE FUN WAY

When I learned how to play basketball, I only knew of certain players who I saw on TV in the 1990s. Scottie Pippen, Michael Jordan, Kobe Bryant, Chamique Holdsclaw and Kim Perrot; just to name a few. If you would've asked me about any other players before that time, I was clueless. One day on my own, I studied who created the game of basketball.

All I can say is that millennials have an amazing advantage with YouTube and social media. Anyone can research anything related to basketball. In my era, I had to wait for the NBA Hardwood Classics to come on ESPN, go to a public library to check a few books out or get information from my parents and grandparents about basketball. So with that being said, the younger ones who are reading this book, it's easier for you guys to find information about basketball games and statistics of current/former basketball players than it was for us.

Let's all do a Challenge!

Many people already know who created the game of basketball. For those who don't have awareness of the origin of the game of basketball; here are some questions for you to answer. Let this be a guide for you on the path of learning more about the game of basketball and who created it.

1. Who created Basketball? _____
_____

2. Where was it created? _____
_____
_____
_____

3. Why was it created? _____
_____
_____
_____

4. The person who created basketball, Does he/she still make a difference in the game today? _____
_____
_____
_____

Please fill in the blanks above for your record. You can also email us your responses at JenarieMiddleton@yahoo.com I would love to know them.

> Also write down on a separate sheet of paper your favorite player and favorite team. Include a top 20 List of your All-Time Favorite Men and Women Players as well.

> If you can meet a current or former Collegiate or Professional Player, Who would that person be? _____
_____
_____

For the last 20 plus years, I've learned so much from watching other great players. I used to study their on-the-court ability by watching games from their college years. I saw how they transitioned into the NBA and WNBA. Even when they competed in the Olympic Games as Amateurs and Professional Athletes, each player who exceeded their talents to the next level taught me that with hard work, practice and determination; success will follow.

However, successful athletes off the court accomplishments rolled over into their everyday lives. Athletes can be more than just players. They can be doctors, lawyers, civil and social leaders. Taking nothing away from their athletic abilities, basketball players will have great duties to fill off the court too. (Once a baller always a baller) Remember where you came from and who lead you to become who you are today. Your parents and close family members are vital to your success. Let their life be a lesson for you. It will save you steps.

For those who do not have a healthy at home situation and seek for outside influence(s), please find mentors and teachers who are there for you. Find mentors that will provide great advice and who will steer you in the right direction. Never let peer pressure and your stubbornness be your downfall. Whatever you do, **STAY FOCUSED** and above all just chill and **HAVE FUN**... You're only a kid once.

10. 🏀
ACRONYM FOR BALLERS 4 L.I.F.E.

Here's an Acronym below to help you Stay Focused and never giving up in L.I.F.E. Our goal is to steer young student-athletes to become responsible and confident leaders of tomorrow on and off the court. This book is a platform to give encouragement where encouragement is lacking. Learning the game of basketball shouldn't always take forced repetition, but it should embody love and endurance to any community everywhere.

**LEARNING**   **FOREVER**

**INTEGRITY**   **EMPOWERING**

11. 🏀
HAVING FUN BEING A BASKETBALLER

My Daughter titled this last chapter. Initially, I wasn't sure what her definition for a basketballer would be, but this is what she had to say.

"A Basketballer is a person that plays basketball and loves basketball and never gives up and keeps going. They practice with basketball and they are good at basketball." ~Janae' Middleton

A phenomenal woman named: Dr. Maya Angelou's paternal grandmother once said to her, "When you get, give. When you learn, teach. These are lessons to live by." As I watched her on Oprah Winfrey's Network 'OWN,' she appeared on Master Class and explained her life story and described what kept her motivated to become someone greater who she never thought to be. It was at that point I fell in love with her grandmother's words. Dr. Maya Angelou has absolutely and most definitely enlightened me to become a better person off the court. She has influenced me in so many areas of my life. Something that I wish I embodied on the court when I played competitively.

I want you all to know that life is wonderful, even in the most difficult times. Life is a way to express your love for others and express your love in the things that brings you joy the most. If you like basketball and look forward to learning it, PLEASE have an open mind and educate yourself on the foundation of its beginning. Anything you desire in life, you must work hard to achieve your goals. Success can be rewarding when you actually take the time to accomplish it. We truly appreciate you for reading this book. Please STAY FOCUSED in this world through Faith, Family and Love.

🏀 Basketball Terminology 🏀

🏀 **Ball Hold:** To hold the ball without the other player taking it away from you. Firmly hold the ball in the triple threat position before taking a shot.

🏀 **Boxing Out/Closing Out:** To position yourself between your opponent and the basket. Not allowing the other player to get the rebound.

🏀 **Box Out/Front Your Man:** In order to box out your opponent, this is where you position yourself between them and the basket. Boxing out is the position you're fighting for before jumping to get the rebound. Fronting your man is when you defend the basket by placing yourself in front of your opponent. In this position, your job is to fight to get in front of the offensive post player. In order to seal your body in front of them, keep your back straight, arms up and knees slightly bent.

🏀 **Brick:** After a rough shot or layup attempt, where the ball hits the backboard or rim hard. A missed shot.

🏀 **Defense:** Not allowing your opponent to score. Preventing the other team from scoring and stopping them from getting their own rebound(s).

🏀 **Defensive Slide:** Bending your knees, keeping your back straight and sliding your feet side to side (from Left to Right).

🏀 **Dribbling:** Patting the ball with your fingertips and bouncing the ball without using the palm of your hand.

🏀 **Jump Shot:** A shot taken in mid-air at the top of your jump.

🏀 **Passing the Ball:** Aiming and directing the basketball at a target on the court, using one or two hands.

🏀 **Patting the Ball:** (See Dribbling)

🏀 **Pump Fake:** When the offensive player pretends to shoot the ball.

🏀 **Rebounding:** Obtaining the ball in your possession after a missed shot.

🏀 **Triple Threat Position:** A position where a player can predetermine their move in different ways. Whether they decide to shoot, pass or dribble. Depending on what they see in front of them.

🏀 **Basketball Half Court Diagram: The Names and Spots on the Basketball Court** 🏀

To increase your on the court basketball knowledge, study these terms on the diagram below:

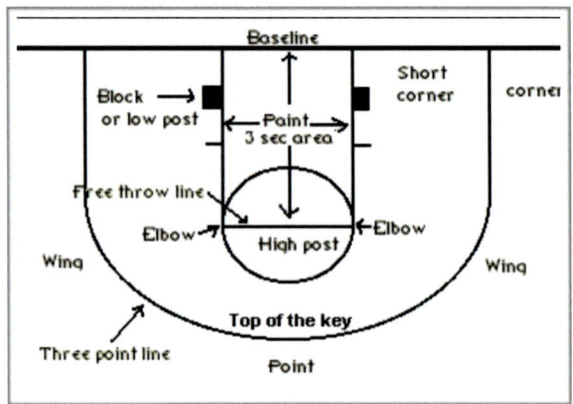

 Basketball and Modesty

This section is for young girls who are modest and who are seeking to play basketball. When I played ball as a kid and in my early adult years, I wasn't modest. In recent years I took on the beauty of modesty. My belief with modesty centers my spirit. Being covered allows me to be humble and meek. Modesty is considered being weird in the black community (I'm speaking on my experience only). Once I became modest, some of my family and friends questioned me, "Why I changed my dress?" My reasoning came from scriptures in the Bible. For instance, 1 Corinthians 12:23: "And on those parts of the body that we think less honorable we bestow the greater honor, and our unpresentable parts are treated with greater modesty." Scriptures like this lead me to become modest. There are so many girls out there who are modest and fear that they won't be accepted as an athlete while being covered. In basketball, some uniforms are revealing. As a covered girl, showing too much of your skin or hair can be intimidating.

I'm here to tell you that it's ok to be comfortable with being yourself. It's ok to go to practice with a long skirt on or tights under your shorts. It's completely fine to cover your head too. Basketball isn't your life. It's just a part of your life for a time. Never allow someone to dictate to you how your modesty should be. Be direct with people in your approach. When you instruct your peers and coaches about your beliefs, be straightforward and be respectful. You don't have to be so forceful with your words to prove who you are. Just politely and calmly speak using your voice to stand for you.

Modesty is beautiful! Own it and play in it. Plus, cross your opponent up! Shoot your best shot! Remember to follow through. It's all in the wrist!

And get back on defense. Don't get caught slipping showing off. Be a leader and a team player. Show them you mean business on that court. Just because you're dressed in modesty doesn't mean you're a slouch.

You are a warrior on that court. Leave it all out there. Give it your best. Kobe Bryant and Pistol Pete Maravich did just that. Be hungry and knowledgeable with your potential on and off the court. Help others around you to become thriving individuals. Set the tone and never let up. You have to expel positivity in all that you try to do. No matter what, you hold the key to your success. I believe in you.

Are you Modest Strong? If not, achieve to reach your higher self. Let your light shine.

Best regards,

Jenarie.

References:

Title: The Baffled Parent's Guide to Coaching Youth Basketball / David G. Faucher; Head Coach, Dartmouth College Men's Team. Nomad Communications Copyright (2000).

YouTube: http://youtu.be/q_J-LIS6q3M. Video Game footage of Dirk Nowitzki elbow to the face. NBA Playoffs, Mavericks -vs- Spurs Game 4. (2001).

Oprah Winfrey's Network - Oprah's Master Class; Dr. Maya Angelou: "Love Liberates." YouTube: http://youtu.be/d7dxnQQEpXs

Title: NBA Basketball Basics / Mark Vancil; Copyright (1995). NBA Properties, Inc.

Website: Coachesclipboard.net; Article, Basketball Fundamentals – Outside (Perimeter) Guard Moves and Skills. By James Gels, from the Coach's Clipboard Basketball Playbook, @ http://www.coachesclipboard.net. Perimeter moves when you have the ball. (Triple threat position) and basketball diagram.

Movie: "The Long Kiss Goodnight." Staring Gina Davis and Samuel L. Jackson; Released by New Line Cinema on October 11, 1996. https://www.youtube.com/watch?v=Jnd06LWlql4&feature=share

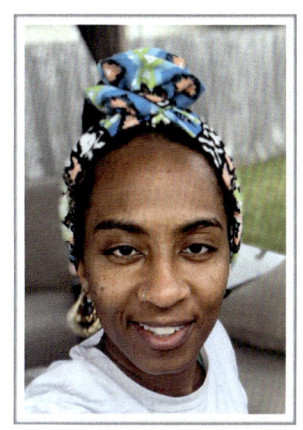

🏀 BONUS FEATURE 🏀
HOW I GOT MY START PLAYING BALL AND HOW IT LEAD ME TO EARN A BASKETBALL SCHOLARSHIP

As a young child, I was very active. My mother always described how I used to flip and do splits in my pampers. She got tired of me recklessly flipping around the house and put me in gymnastics class. Eventually, I went on to be a good runner too. I wasn't the fastest, but I was long-winded. Although I never performed or competed with kids in my age group, I was good enough naturally to play and run with them. In both sports, I did well. However, in gymnastics, I did exceptionally well. We lived in Queens, NY and the first gym I performed at was in Rockville Center. I eventually moved to another gym located in Brooklyn. There I trained with Romanian coaches and went on to earn my spot competing with (14 and 16-year-olds). The pace was different and the training style was really intense. We had to do 50 push-ups before we started practice and we all stretched together in a group. Our stretching techniques were unorthodox. It was pilates, yoga, and calisthenics all wrapped in one. I remember witnessing plenty of girls quitting on the spot because they couldn't handle the drastic workouts. We all cried and we all experienced tough love from our Romanian coaches. Their names were, Mike and Rodika. They looked like they were between the ages of 50-60 years old and they exuded so much passion for teaching gymnastics. At the time I didn't understand the magnitude of their instruction. When I initially came to the gym I was 6 years old. I began practicing at level 4. Almost overnight, I quickly progressed to level 6. After competing in a few gymnastics meets, my performance caught Mike and Rodika's attention. They decided to move me up again from

Level 6 on to level 8. I had just turned 7 years old and was going to compete with the 10 and 11-year-olds.

The scrutiny I experienced impacted my self-esteem. I would show up early for practice to join my new teammates and instead of them welcoming me, they pretend as if I wasn't there. Since they shunned me, I turned my attention toward the 14-year-olds to build my confidence. I studied their moves by watching them do their routines. In deep thought, I pondered on how I could reach their level. All of my teammates at my level thought I was showboating. They began to purposely ostracized me. At first, it got to me, but then I realized that I was from South Jamaica Queens. My community was a middle class urban/suburban neighborhood. There were so many cultures of people I was surrounded by. I saw more minorities than I did white people. The gym I transferred to was in a community full of Italians and Jewish people. There was nothing we had in common. No matter how hard I tried to communicate with them and build with them, they shut me out. Leaving me there alone to fend for myself. Not all of my teammates treated me badly though. The ones I was closer to shared commonalities with me. My coaches noticed that I wasn't fitting in. They took me under their wing and began to give me more individual time. When I came to practice instead of joining my peers, I had to learn techniques that were newer and harder. Falling was becoming repetitive. I used to fall down a lot. My coaches were stern and they would say, "Come on, get up. Get up now and keep going." I used to cry and I used to feel bad, but I never quit! I took those hard falls and

pushed through the pain. I felt scared every time I learned new routines. Especially routines on the balance beam and uneven bars. I'd sit up there on the top bar looking down at everyone. I was so much higher than them.

To face my fears, I'd look over toward Mike with concern, and without hesitation, his response was always a pat on my behind, a grab to my chin and a gruntled loud voice, "Up Now, let's go!" When I finally got the nerve to continue, I just closed my eyes and trusted that he'd spot me and guide me. No matter how frightened I was, I persevered. My landings at first were sloppy and weak. Over time they became stronger and firm. With every accomplishment, I received backlash from my teammates. It left me feeling hopeless and sad. However, I used my talent as a gymnast to overshadow how they treated me.

Within a year I was competing with the 16-year-olds at level 9. My practices were serious. More serious than my peers in my age group. The Olympics was coming to Atlanta, Georgia in another year, but I was only 10 years old. Even though I had so much excitement and was so eager, I had to wait for the 2000 Olympics. My coaches asked my parents for their permission to take me to their home country in Romania to train there. I was so thrilled to hear about their invite. My favorite athlete at the time was Dominiques Dawes. When she trained for the 1988 and 1992 Olympics, she had moved in with her coaches. I watched a special about how she trained and I screamed, "Mommy!" My mother came running up the stairs in a panic. She was like, "What? What happened? What's wrong?" I replied saying, "I'm ready to train for the Olympics." She looked at me and was like, "The 96' Olympics? I said, "No the 2000 Olympics." I will be old enough to compete. Plus I can go to Romania and train with Mike and Rodika. She paused real quick saying, "Well I don't know about that. We're gonna have to have a family meeting about that one. Plus we don't have money for you to travel all the way over there. And who's gonna watch you?" I told her with so much poise. "I can take care of myself." She looked back at me saying, "Girl please!" I was really serious and she thought I was trippin'. I wanted to prove to her and to my family that I wanted this badly. I went to practice with another set of eyes and mindset. No matter what was going on around me, nothing could take my mind off of the Olympics. My mother discussed everything with my family and they all concluded to allow me to go. There was a catch though. The catch was, that my mother will travel with me and Rodika. As long as I was responsible for maintaining my grades, they agreed to raise money for me so I could go. This was my time to prove to everyone that my talent meant something. It meant that I could use the talent The Creator gave me. I felt compelled to make a difference for other young black girls like me. To show them that they too can pursue their passion, no matter where they come from and no matter what circumstances they were facing. My goal was to show them that they can make it.

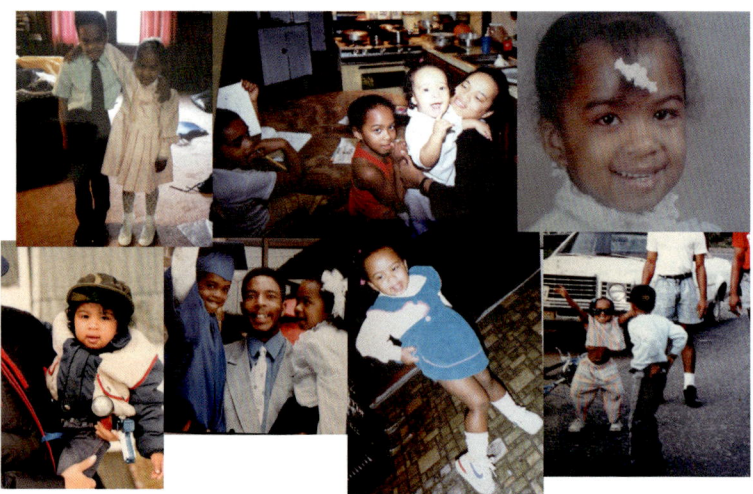

# It All Came Tumbling Down

You know that expression people say, "It hit me like a ton of bricks?" Well, I felt those words differently this time around. My mother came to me and said, "You're not going to Romania to train." We were in the car on our way back home from practice. She stopped by a Bodega to get me my favorite hero sandwich. Then I put my head on the back of the passenger seat. I looked out the front windshield in disbelief. Feeling disappointed, I turned and asked, "But why mommy? Why can't I go? Is it the money?" She replied saying, "No, not really." My comeback was, "Then what's the issue mommy? Didn't Rodika tell us that she's coming with us? She won't lead us wrong!" My mother gave me a brief lesson about our social and worldly events. She asked me if I knew anything about the war in Romania. She further explained that it was not the best time for me to go train over there. Another thing she mentioned was that my coaches only wanted me to go without her. She said to me, "HELL NO, you're not going over there without me. It'll be other times. They're other coaches you can train with besides Mike and Rodika. Don't be so upset." I was devastated and silent the whole ride home. Believe it or not, I was ranked #20 in the state and just started practicing at level 10. This was my passion and all I wanted to do was compete.

Not too long after getting bad news about not being able to go to Romania, my parents informed us with some more surprising news. That we are moving to Florida. I was like, "Florida! What's in Florida besides Disney World?" In my mind back then any state beyond South Carolina was weird. I was used to traveling to SC because that's where my family originated, but not to Florida!

My school year ended, gymnastics season was just starting and we were moving to another state. I told myself that I was done with gymnastics. How will I start over in a new city, with new coaches? My parents reassured me that I'd find a place to train. We left NY in July of 1995 and I started an all year round school that very next week. I was saddened because I thought we were only going to live in Florida for the summer. Nope, we were here to stay. The cultural dynamic in Florida was so unusual. Nothing seemed right. The way people talked, the way they wore their clothes, everything was different and I was so bored. Back at home, I had gymnastics to keep me focused. Our reality was new to me and I had no choice but to adapt.

My parents found a gymnastics facility to train in and all of a sudden I got that unwelcoming feeling again. That same feeling I had in New York when my teammates ignored me. I had to prove myself all over again. I hated every practice I went to. I despised being ostracized. I didn't want to keep feeling like this. These repeated dreams of me flipping non-stop kept waking me up from my sleep at night. One day I came home and told my parents that I didn't want to pursue gymnastics anymore. I told them that I was done with it. I just wanted to be a regular kid. From the ages of (4-9), I competed. There were times when I wouldn't come home until 11 pm from practice. I needed a break. So they told me, "If this is what you really want, we will respect your decision."

🏀 My New Passion 🏀

After one year in sunny Florida, things got better. I met new friends and was entering the 6th grade. With gymnastics behind me, I wasn't thinking about sports. The only thing that I thought about was being a kid and having fun. All the girls who were athletic in my grade played basketball, volleyball, soccer, softball and ran track. I was a little intimidated. I was only great at flipping and running long

distances. Back in NY, I was the only athlete in my class. The competition was steep here. If I wanted to play sports, I had to step my game up. Unfortunately, I didn't know what new sport to choose from. One day in gym class, we had to participate in doing different activities with our team groups. We tried all sports. The first sport I remember our groups competed in was Volleyball and I instantly hated it. First of all, it was too many of us trying to play. We all couldn't get it together. Most of us who didn't like playing stood closer to the net or on the sidelines. I knew that was a fail. Then we played soccer next. I was feeling soccer! I had a thing for kicking the ball and dribbling it with my feet and knees. I took it seriously, but everyone else was like, "Nah, this is a no go." A week later, we moved on to softball. Softball wasn't too bad, but I hated how slow it was. Plus I wanted to throw the ball like a baseball and not underhanded. So yeah, that was a dump too. Gym class was always fun because we had a chance to connect without having to be stuck in a classroom all day long.

The last sport we played was basketball. Aw man let me tell you how shaken up I was. I never played basketball in my life. I shot a ball a few times when I was younger. I even watched the 90's NBA era games too. I had no clue how to hold the ball, pass the ball, shoot the ball, nothing! I felt so shy. We had to play as a team in front of the entire gym class. I was rooting everyone on to play as long as I didn't get on the court, then I was cool with it. The coach called time out and subbed me in. My eyes got so big. I was shaking in my boots, bad! lol, 😂 I went in and we played defense first. Surprisingly, I did pretty well. My footwork and coordination from track and gymnastics paid off. I was sliding my feet, staying in front of my opponent and my nervousness went away.

I was on cloud nine for maybe 10 seconds. As soon as the possession switched and it was our time to score, I froze dead in my tracks. Somebody threw me the ball and I ducked. I literally ducked. Man, I looked up and everybody was laughing at me. Man, you suck! Dang, Social suicide just began.

7th Grade

6th grade went by fast. I played around and procrastinated a lot in math class and failed. I got my last report card in the mail and it read, RETAINED! The summer of 1997, I took a math class so I can be promoted to the 7th grade. Thankfully I passed. It was actually fun going to summer school. I met some people who attended other schools and their personalities matched mine. They didn't seem to be heavily involved in their academics. They just wanted to come to class and finish their work so they can move on. This was the year I learn how to fail. Failing isn't normal in the school system.  Once you failed you are then labeled as someone who cannot do the work. I told myself that although I didn't have a passing grade, I won't let this damper my capabilities. I am not a failure! I will do better and I will succeed no matter what people label me as.

Seventh Grade starts and it's a new year. I pretty much saw the same classmates from the previous year. Nothing drastically changed. I was in my 2nd year playing in the band. I was in first chair playing the clarinet. Sometimes I would lose my chair to move to fourth chair for disciplinary reasons. I used to talk a lot and my band instructor, Mr. Duran would take my first chair status away from me. After class one day I asked him, "I worked hard to become first chair, Why did you move me to fourth chair?" He said, "Jenarie, to continue to be great, there will be times when you have to step up. When you have to be mature. There are consequences to your behavior. If I allow you to keep disrupting my class, you will be a hindrance to yourself and the rest of your bandmates." He explained, "Now you can get your chair back when you earn it. Have a great day and see you tomorrow." I was so upset and left that conversation puffed up and angry. I had time to walk back to my next class to cool off. After lunch that day I got over it. The next day I started in fourth chair. People laughed at me and said, "Dang Jenarie, you're way in fourth chair?" I took their criticism and made it my business to get back to being first chair. Mr. Duran didn't let up either. He kept his word and left me there. Eventually I did earn my first chair back. I failed because of my attitude, but I gained knowledge with my failure. After passing my solo performances and outplaying my chair section, I got my first chair status back.

I carried this competitiveness over into my other classes and sports. I started paying attention in class. Then I made A/B Honor Roll and I got involved with being my better self. It was all working out.

Remember when I told you how sorry I was? How a few of my friends told me that I sucked? Hearing them say that never left me. "You Suck!," was my new name on the court. Sometimes it even traveled with me down the halls. "Aye Jenarie, man you suck!" They would be laughing exceedingly. At first, it used to bother me and I would go home feeling sad about it. I'd stare in the mirror and say to myself, "Do I really suck that bad?" With a deep sigh, I'll tell myself that I probably do suck.

The day of tryouts was slowly approaching. I told my Dad that I wanted to play basketball. He was like, "You want to play ball? Are you sure?" In the back of my mind, I'm like I don't even know if I could, but I said yes anyway. He told me, "If I show you how to play, don't make me waste my time if you're not serious." I said, "Yes daddy I'm ready." He said, "Show me what you can do." I looked at him and said show you what? What do you mean? He slapped his forehead and said, "Oh goodness. Jenarie Do you know what offense and defense is?" I said, "No, what is that?" It's like my responses were his kryptonite. Before he slapped his head in disbelief, now he just rested his hands on his knees and dropped his head. lol

He said, "Ok since you don't understand the basics of basketball, let me show you how to defend the ball." Now mind you, we had no basketball. He was just showing me how to dribble without anything in his hands. He told me, "I don't care whose dribbling the ball in front of you. You can steal the ball away from anyone." I asked him how? He said, "Timing! You must time the ball. If you can time the ball, then you can make it on that team. Never mind your offense, it's your defense that's going seal the deal. What you have to do is, watch the ball and watch their hips simultaneously. You have to have good eye coordination. Once the ball leaves their hands, that's it. It's nothing but air and opportunity. It will take time for that ball to bounce back up to their hand. They have no control over the ball once it leaves their hands. When you time the ball coming back up from the ground, that's your time to swipe the ball away from them." We practiced timing the ball for hours until he got tired. He said, "Alright, that's your lesson. Now go make the team." When daddy went back in the house I felt good. I was a little worried because I was hoping that he would teach me more about offense and shooting, but he didn't.

Tryouts came and oh my goodness, guys I was so worried I couldn't even take the pressure. Everybody who laughed at me who said I sucked was like, "Look she's here to try out." They kept on laughing. I shook it off and said to myself you got this Nay. (I am affectionately known as Nay-Nay) So the coaches outlined the tryouts by sections. The first section was endurance. I did that easily. Now the shooting and passing drills came. Everyone shot the ball and passed it great. They passed me the ball and I barely caught it. I took no dribbles and then shot the ball. It went over the basket, touching nothing. The coaches were like, "Wow! Ok! Next!" Yeah, I knew that was horrible. The next section was passing. The coaches said, "Please pass the ball to your teammate." It was my turn. As soon as I passed the ball it went into the bleachers. Everybody was laughing and smirking like dang She Sucks! I went towards the back of the line feeling like a small ant. Like, Why Am I even here? I know I'm never gonna make the team now.

The last section was defense. My eyes got big and I immediately felt excited. I said to myself, Daddy went over this with me. I can do this!" So it was my turn to defend the ball. The coaches were not impressed with me thus far and their facial expressions were showing it. They blew the whistle and I defended the ball. Every time they tried to dribble I stole the ball. No one couldn't get passed me. Instead of the coaches telling me to get in the back of the line, they kept switching offensive players and continued to have me play defense. No one could pass me. We took our water break and they announced that tomorrow afternoon we'll have the final roster posted on the girls' locker room door. Good luck lady's and have a great night. I came home and told my mom about the tryouts, but at the time back then she used to work long hours and kind of paid it no mind. She told me, "Let me know if you made it tomorrow when you get home from school." I said, ok. The next day came and all day I was full of butterflies. It wasn't the end of the day yet so the roster wasn't posted. When the last bell rang I rushed out of class so quick. Running passed everyone to see if I made the team. I went out back to get my bicycle and when I arrived to the locker room, everyone who did make the team was happy and giving high-fives to each other. I saw a few girls who were disappointed. That let me know they didn't make the team. I went up to the door and waited for my turn. I scrolled my fingers down the list and there it was. My Name, "Jenarie Davis!" I jumped up so high and screamed out, "Yes, Yes! I can't believe I actually made the team." There wasn't any practice that day, so I got on my bike and rode home fast to share the news with my parents. This time my dad was home so he was there to hear the news too.

I raddled the keys in the door so much I was shaking trying to open the door. Mommy, Daddy Guess what? They said, "What?" I replied, "I made the team. I actually made the team!" My mom was so thrilled for me. She hugged and kissed me. Daddy said, "I told you didn't I. If you can defend the ball, then you can make that team. Now the real work begins." Now I had to practice playing my clarinet and practice playing ball. All while being a student and a big sister. At the time I didn't think about it. My nerves were on cloud nine to even think that far.

I finished the remaining of the basketball season as a bench rider. Because I could barely dribble, I only came in the games to defend the ball. Every time I stole or deflected the ball, I'd stand there waiting for someone to come get the ball from me. How pathetic right? When school was finished my parents thought it was good that we spend the entire summer in New York. Two years had gone by since we moved here and my brother and grandparents were missing us. We arrived in NY and about 3 weeks went by and all we did was stay in the house or played outside together. It was my siblings and my two cousins. My brother and I were the oldest. We were 13 and 12 and everyone else was 7 and under. One rainy day, my Nanna asked us what it is that we liked to do? She is an avid community leader and expected that we do extracurricular activities. Sitting on idol time was something we just couldn't do on her watch. That day my Uncle Randy asked me if I wanted to play basketball. I reluctantly said yes. I was scared to play ball up there. New York was the Mecca of basketball. If they thought I sucked back home, I knew they would think I was trash up here.

We drove to Roy Wilkins Park Community Center off of Merrick and Foch Blvd. My uncle asked that if it were any spots left for me to join the summer camp. The office coordinator replied quickly saying, "No. All of our spots are filled to capacity. Sorry!" We left and my uncle told me, "Don't even worry about it. We will find a way for you to play. You may not be able to be apart of the camp, but you will make it on the team. In the meantime, we have to get you a ball so you can practice your dribbling because niece with all due respect your handles suck!" Dang, even my own uncle said I sucked. It had to be true then. Lol.

my great grandmother, (my Nanna's mother), Sarah Williams took me to JCPenny and bought me my first basketball. The WNBA first season started that summer in May 1998 and I asked if I could get a WNBA basketball. She said, "If that's what you want, then yes. Is it anything else you wanted?" I rarely asked for things that I wanted so when she asked me if I wanted something else, I quickly said yes. I had my eyes on the New York Liberty Jersey's and The Houston Comets Jersey's. I chose Teresa Weatherspoon (NYL) and Cynthia Cooper (HC) Jersey's. They were my favorite players. She told me, "Make sure you take care of those jerseys. Don't just leave them in the closet. Make sure you wear them." I said, "Oh you won't have to worry about that Monda. (Monda is what we affectionately called her) I'm gonna wear these every chance I get."

My uncle gave me a workout plan to do every day until the summer was over. He said, "Your goal is to be better than you are now. To go back home and to become a starter on your 8th-grade team." I thought he was too far fetched. How Am I going to be able to do that? I didn't have a choice, so whatever drills he gave me, I had to do them. These are the drills below:

- Dribble with your left hand only, from the house all the way to Roy Wilkins Park. (To get to the park from my grandparent's house, It took 20 minutes)

- Jog while you dribble.

- When you shoot say, How ya Doin'!

- Find a group of boys to play with.

- Play defense by sliding your feet and watching their hips.

- Run the court.

- Pass the ball.

- Be willing to take a hit and get back up.

- 50 push-ups a day.

I remember him going over everything with me and I was feeling nauseous thinking about it. I ask him, "Uncle Randy, How am I going to do all of this on my own? Why can't you come with me?" He replied saying, "I have to watch the younger kids. There will be days when I can come with you, but most times I'll be at the house with them. You have to learn how to do things on your own. If you think someone is going to be there for you all the time, then I would be setting you up for failure. To succeed and get better, you have to learn on your own." So there I was walking and jogging every day up to the park. My brother had to tag along with me, but sometimes he would veer off with his friends. I had to force myself to talk to other kids. I wasn't a talker and was introverted. To talk to people was like pulling teeth. It just wasn't for me. However, for me to progress, I had to step out of my comfort zone.

Within no time my skills were beginning to change. It was noticeable. The kids at the park labeled me as, "That Girl." Instead of asking to play next, I was becoming one of the regular ballers. I didn't have to introduce myself anymore. Later my uncle ran into the summer league coach and asked if I could play with the team. It was  no more camp spots, but she had an extra shirt and allowed me to play. I was officially a part of the Rifle Ball Team.

My first game was coming up and I wanted my Nanna and Granddaddy to come see me play. My Granddaddy was like, "Girl you can't play. I ain't coming if you can't play." I said with confidence, "Granddaddy trust me, I can play!"

So there they all were my Nanna, Granddaddy, Uncle Randy, my brother, sisters and cousins. They were standing at the gate waiting for the game whistle to blow. I was so nervous because this was my test. This game would solidify whether I was good or not. The game began. We played defense first. Everything was running smooth. I played defense at the top of the key and I stole the ball and dribbled back, laying the ball up on my right-hand side. All I can hear is my

Uncle Randy scream, "That's what I'm talkin' bout' Nay!" We ended up winning the game. Everyone was so happy for me. Granddaddy even said, "Ok Nay you can play."

We had many games left, but the game I remember most was the game we played at The WNBA and The NBA Cares Community Event at Roy Wilkins Park. I met <u>Kym Hampton</u> from the New York Liberty and <u>Anthony Mason</u> of the New York Knicks. There were so many games being played on four different courts. When it was our turn to play, for some reason, everyone centered their attention on our game instead.

Tip-off got going and it was our possession. The first play of the game was a cross over move by my teammate. Her move was so potent that everyone gasped and said, "OMG!" Right after, that our opponents came across the half-court line. I stole the ball and saw that we were in a 2 on 1 possession. I did a no-look pass to my teammate, she passed it right back to me and I passed it between my legs behind me to my other teammate and she (Shot), layed the ball up, scoring. When sports announcers use the term, "The crowd went wild." I mean people were clapping as if we were in a championship game.

When the game was over, Anthony Mason came up to me and said, "Miss lady, you held your own out there. Keep Ballin!" I was jumping up and down inside my body so much, but my face was calm. My Uncle Randy was like, "Yo Kid, Who are you? This can't be the same Nay-Nay who couldn't dribble a few weeks ago!"For the rest of the summer, I felt more poised and gained wisdom. I gained friends and independence. I knew what it took to be better. Not just on the court, but off the court too.

It was time to come back home to Florida. We made it back safely on the first day of school. We arrived early that morning. We unpacked and went straight to school from there. When people asked me how my summer was I told them that I just got back this morning. I missed New York, but I had business to take care of this year. After a great summer, the basketball season came again. When tryouts were held my coaches and classmates noticed a difference in my game. I still had to prove myself to become a starter. Our third game we played was against Southside Middle School. I came off the bench that game. We were down a few points and I told myself, "Nay if you get in the game play smart, work with your team and ball out!" I did just that. We won that game and I scored 15 points. From that game on, I became a starter. That season went 10-1 and we were league champions!

The summer of 1998 was the best summer ever. I went into my 8th grade year full of tenacity and the will to persevere. My grades improved dramatically and I completed Middle School with a bang. My ninth grade year started with summer school. My mother didn't want me to sit home all day. She told me, "You're going to summer school at Wolfson." (Wolfson was the name of my High School) I looked at her crazy and said, "Summer School? But Ma, I wasn't retained! I did well with my grades." Total opposite from the end of my sixth grade school year. She explained saying, "I don't want you sitting around at home doing nothing. They are allowing a few incoming ninth graders to take a few classes during the summer and you're going." At first I thought, Why is she doing this to me? I sat there on the couch and said, "My whole summer is over!"

My mother registered me to take Earth Space Science, with Coach Frank Jenkins. At the time I didn't have a clue who he was. My mother said, "Go in there and make the best of this science class. Don't start High School off on a bad note."

When the first day of class started, I recognized a few people from middle school. It didn't seem as bad once I saw my classmates. After spending two weeks in the classroom, I saw Coach Jenkins walking towards the gym. I asked if I could come in and shoot for a while. He said, "Yes." He was expecting a few players to come in and shoot around. It was a few girls I recognized who played for my middle school who were two years ahead of me. They were top notch ballers. I was intimidated by them for sure.

After a few times coming to the gym, Coach Jenkins asked three of us if we wanted to play for his Summer League Team. I told him, "I'd love to play I just have to ask my parents first." I went home and told my mom that my science teacher was the Girls Varsity Basketball Coach. She said, "I already knew that. What I didn't know about was the basketball summer league. She said, "Let me talk with your father to see if it's ok first. You're already running track, How are you going to multitask summer track and summer basketball?" I looked at her and shrugged my shoulders. I told her, "Well, you told me that I shouldn't be lounging around. To not sit on idol time. Right?" She turned her head and had the death stare. I sat and waited to see what she'd do or say next. She breathed heavily and squeezed her lips together and said, "Don't play with me." I jokingly said, "Mommy, please I'm so sorry. I'm just saying what you told me a few weeks ago." I reassured her that I would manage my time right and I would be responsible. She told me that I had to continue helping out around the house. Completing my chores, cooking dinner for my sisters and doing good in school. I promised her that I'd hold it down, and I did.

Our first summer league game drew near. I was nervous, because I never competed against High School Girls, let alone High School Juniors and Seniors. Some of the players from my school didn't join our summer league team, because they participated with their AAU teams. So we went up against, "Sistas Wit Game." A well known, talented girls team from my city in Jacksonville, FL. We were like the underdogs and they were the elite squad. Remember, that movie, "Little Giants," yeah we were them. Going up against the Cowboys. I knew we were not going to win. The final score was 110-10. I scored 8 points. We couldn't even get the ball passed half court. Every time we tried to pass, shoot or dribble, it was like we were babies and they were taking the candy away from us.

They kept laughing, scoring and destroying us! Man our ego was shot to the ground beneath us. Some people who started playing with us, never came back to play with our team after that game. It left us with only six players. I felt so embarrassed. My mother was there to witness our brutal beating. After the game was over, I overheard players from our side say, "Man we sorry, I ain't coming back." I shook my head. I really wanted to cry right where I stood, but I held it in. My mother stopped me as I was walking out of the gym. She said, "Sometimes we have to fail, to know how to win. Don't let this loss get you down. Let this loss be the fuel that ignites your passion. You won't be low for long. I believe in you." As I write this, it's like I'm looking into her eyes all over again with 13 year old eyes. I shed a few tears and she wiped them saying, "Don't let nobody see you crying either. Hold your head up strong. You got this. Now let's go home."

 No Matter What Stay Focused

 Persevere

 Believe In Yourself

 Practice

 Endure

 Learn The Game

 Never Give Up

 Feel The Game Within You

 Ask Questions

 Rest When You Can

 Eat Healthy

 Gain Academic and Real World Knowledge

Summer Activities Coming To An End

The last game we had ton play was at Ribault High School. We had to play Bishop Kenny. The game started at 5:30pm I believe and my summer track AAU team had practice right down the street at Raines High School. It was a two hour practice and it was scorching outside. The practice was awkward that day, because I no longer wanted to train for the hurdles. My coach was a little disappointed, because he saw the potential I had for that event. I wanted to concentrate on other areas, so that I wouldn't burn myself out. Going from a two hour basketball session to a two hour track practice was getting to me.

Track practice was over with, now it was time for me to go to Ribault and play these girls. For some reason that day I really wanting to win. It was another team that played before we did. I was resting and drinking some water and decide to pray. I asked The Creator that he give me strength. Strength to help my team win and for me to play at my best ability. After this game we were heading back to New York for a week before 9th grade started. So I wanted to leave with this last game as a winner.

As we warmed up, I noticed that the Bishop Kenny Coach was a little antsy. She was a lot more serious than my coach was. I told myself that if we can take control of this game, she will lose her composer. I found her weakness. We huddled up and Coach Jenkins told us what he said, the entire summer league. "Feel the game and let it come to you. Play smart and play together." We ended the huddle and walked away. Tip off started and the game began. It was a heated battle from jump. My teammate Nikki and I was on fire. We were playing like Joe Dumars and Isaiah Thomas from The Detroit Pistons. Every time they tried to press us in the back court we'd break their press. Their coach was getting mad. One of her players was talking trash to us and said some derogatory words. After so many times of hearing this I was beginning to get frustrated. However, I kept my composure and focused on the game instead. After a few more possessions, this one girl wouldn't let up. She was overly irritated when she couldn't get passed our defense. Then she pushed me. Then I walked up to her and pushed her back. At this point the gym is going crazy. I just knew they were going to kick us out the game. But they called a technical foul on the both of us. My coach was yelling at the Referee. Then he grabbed me by my jersey and said, "Jenarie get over here now!" Aw man, I done messed up now! I sat on the bench concerned, because I thought he was gonna rip me to shreds. But he didn't. He said, "Jenarie, that's what I'm talking about.

That's the way to show passion! Now let's run this play." We all huddled up and went back out on that floor for more. It's like that possession was the fuel to my ignition my mother told me about from our first game of the season. So this is what she was talking about. Oh I'm ready now.

It's our ball and we have to start from the sideline closets to the other team's bench. As I dribbled the ball on the sideline passed my defender, their coach raised her foot out towards me. Thinking that she could trip me. But guess what frustrated coach, (Aht Aht), I hurdled right over her leg. The people in the stands saw what she did and everyone was in an uproar. At this

point this game wasn't going to end peacefully. No matter who wins, the winner will have bragging rights indeed.

We won the game! We walked over to the sideline to shake hands and the other team was super salty, but whatever!

My coach was so thrilled and happy. He gave us a great speech after the game. The kind of speech that stick with you for years. He told us, "You all played with tremendous heart. No one can't teach you to have those attributes, it must come from within you. I'm so proud of you girls. Have a great summer and I hope to see you all at try outs."

I walked to my mother and siblings and they were so hype. My mom said, "Jenarie, I wanted to go down there and whoop those people butts for you, but you held your own baby. I am so proud of you for facing adversity and conquering. You didn't allow your frustrations to get the best of you and that's what life is all about. Now let's go!"

Ninth Grade is here baby! We made it to the Mecca of Social Suicide. Here's the time where life can make or break you. The same way my eight grade year began was the same for ninth grade. We came back from New York and had to go straight to school. This time school began at 7:15 am and I was not a morning person. I remember walking the halls during the summer, so I didn't feel lost like most of my classmates did. My schedule seemed nice and I was ready to take on this new journey. Basketball season wasn't for a few weeks and I had to make sure my grades were exceptional. In my mind I was preparing for soccer, basketball and track. I

was still playing my clarinet and in the band as well. My father shut it down though. He said, "You're not running us ragged." He told me to only choose one sport. I was so furious. All of my other friends I've been playing with were doing multiple sports, Why couldn't I? Instead of fighting it, I agreed to his wishes and only focused on playing basketball.

Tryouts came and I was ready. It was 4:15 pm and I got on my bike and rode to practice. At the time I lived right across the street from my school. It was easy being able to multitask. I still had to be responsible with helping out at home and being a student athlete. I arrived to tryouts at 4:20pm. I was on the baseline about to begin our drills. Coach Jenkins walked up to me and said, "Why are you here?" I looked back behind me and said, "You talking to me? He said, "Yes! Why didn't you report to practice at 2:15pm?" Everyone is looking at me confused too. I responded to him saying, "Isn't that the Varsity Practice time? He said, "Yes. You don't have to be here. Tomorrow you need to report to our 2:15pm practice and don't be late! You can leave now."I told everyone goodbye and I rode my bike back home. It wasn't even 20 minutes that passed and my mom said, "Why are you here? Tryouts went by that fast?" I told her, "No. Coach Jenkins told me to report to practice tomorrow at 2:15pm." She replied, "But isn't that the varsity practice time? I answered her eagerly, "Yes!" Then she said, "So you are on the varsity team, is that what you're saying?" I guess I am mother.

I remember my first game was at home against Englewood High School. Those same people who said I sucked in middle school watched me play that game. It was an early game that started at 3pm. I scored 18 points.

My freshman year was fun and I learned so much playing with my teammates. I was the youngest on the team and I did my best holding my own on the court. I came from not knowing anything about basketball, to making it on the varsity basketball team in 1 1/2 years. I played with summer AAU teams from Jacksonville, Daytona and Orlando. Most of my practices started in the spring term. Sometimes I had to miss school and report to AAU basketball practice in Orlando. I was reliable and trustworthy enough to travel down there alone on The Greyhound Bus. My parents taught me how to handle myself without them. For two years I'd travel back and forth to Orlando and Daytona. I was the weakest player on my AAU team. The girls I was playing with were raked on Florida's Top Girls Basketball List. I was so out of my league. No matter what I faced and no matter how bad I played I took it as a learning lesson.

I went on to face so much adversity during my high school career. I took responsibility for most of it. I couldn't hang out with my peers or teammates, my parents were very strict and I believe that led me to have little connection with them. Without a real bond off the court, it affected our bond on the court. No matter what, I worked with whatever was given to me. We still played well and did great as a team. The other half of what I experienced was bad timing. Whether I had issues with my grades in school, with personal relationships, with my own teammates and with my coach. My high school experience ended on a bad note.

College

My grades were subpar and my SAT scores were very low. That took a toll on who could recruit me. I had offers from big D1 (Division One) schools but due to having a low test score, I only had a few offers from (JUCCO) community colleges. It was one month left of school and I still didn't decide where I wanted to go yet. I was invited to play at The Citywide Basketball Game, Southside against Northside All-Stars. I was assigned to play with the Southside Team. University Christian Coach coached us. He put me at the point guard position. It didn't matter what position I played in, as long as I played I was fine with it. We won that game and scouts were present. One of the schools I'm familiar with walked up to me to offer me a full scholarship. The School was Seminole Community College. I had only thought about going to my cities community college at the time because it was closer to home. However, because I traveled back and forth to Orlando and Daytona, I felt comfortable going there. My parents insisted that I stay at home. Their package was so influencing. Plus I loved their academic programs. Instead of going there, I decided to stay home and attend Florida Community College. I always tell myself that I should have left home and played away. Staying home really sheltered me in a way. If I had left I probably would have forced myself to stay focused. Knowing that I had my parents to lean on here, I took advantage of it.

# Summer School

I decided to take a few classes before starting the fall semester. I did very well that term and got familiar with my coaches and with the campus. The fall season began and my schedule came. I was scheduled to take six classes that fall. Each class was core classes, no electives. I wasn't used to having so much to handle at once and we still had to have time for practice, for conditioning, for study hall and community service. Ultimately, I flunked my first semester. And it wasn't only me who flunked. It was several of us on the team that was ineligible to play. My GPA was above a 2.0, but I failed to have 12 credit hours. I only had 9. The rules for Junior college states that a student-athlete must have a 2.0 and 12 credit hours to play.

I was so disappointed in myself. How could this have happened? I felt dumb and felt like a failure. I was at my lowest. My Father heard of the news and told me that I'm no longer going to be on the team. My coach stressed that I would still be able to finish my spring semester on scholarship, I just couldn't play or travel with the team. My father wasn't having it. He stated that, "If she failed with her grades then she most definitely won't need basketball. He told her, you are her coach for now, but I'm her coach for life." He stressed that my grades mattered most. He requested that I get a waiver signed so I could focus only on my academics. She reluctantly signed my waiver and that was that. I was no longer a basketball player for any team. My father came home and told me to get a job immediately. I just turned 18 years old and never worked a day in my life. I felt lost. He came to me and said, "You want to know what life is about? Life is not all about sports, what's going to happen if you get hurt and you lose your scholarship. What degree will you have? Life for you begins now."

I started the spring term already feeling defeated. My teammates who decided to stay on the team stopped talking to me. They would walk right passed me on campus like they never knew me. My new goal was to pass my classes and get my GPA up. I thought that playing ball was over. I liked working at my job. I was making and saving my own money. I had a great routine at school and work. Then my father came home and said, "Let's go!" I asked where are we going. He said, "Don't worry about it. Get in the car." As we were riding I was curious to know what he was up to. Daddy wasn't showing any signs of nervousness at all. Everything was fine and normal as can be. Then we stopped at the intersection of Merrill and University Blvd. and I saw the sign, "Jacksonville University." I closed my lips tight and looked at Daddy and asked him, "What are we doing here?"

He drove on campus and parked. He said, "Being that you're no longer on anyone's team and have a signed waiver for you to be released, I called the head coach." I screamed out saying, "Daddy you did what?" I asked him, "Like when and how? She answered your call? How does she know who I am?" He said, "Nay chill. Be quiet. Learning comes from listening." Now my Dad always has a way to get you to listen, but at this point, I wanted to know everything. So I stopped asking questions and opened my ears to listen. He explained to the JU coach that I was no longer playing ball for my school. He mentioned all of my accolades from High School and she remembered who I was. She told him that she was interested in me attending and would look into having me be apart of the team. So as he's talking to me, explaining their conversation, all I kept thinking about was Allen Iverson's Mother. That one time when he was in jail, she contacted the Georgetown Basketball Coach, John Thompson and pleaded his case. She told him to take a chance on her son and believe in his talent. After Allen Iverson served his time, he was later signed to play for the Hoyas. This is why I referred my Dad as Allen Iverson's Mom. All I could think about as we walked down the stairs towards her office was, "Is this real right now?" Right before we entered, my Dad asked me, "Are you ready? I closed my eyes and took a deep breath. I told him, "Yes I'm ready." He said, "Alright, Let's go!"

Man, let me tell you, my heart was pounding you hear me! I mean pumping hard. The coach walked towards me with her hand out saying, "Its a pleasure to finally meet you Jenarie. I remember you playing for Wolfson, number four right!" I was shaking so badly and my voice was quivering, but I still replied with my best response. I told her thanks for admiring my game. I appreciate you. She turned her back towards us, leading us to her office. When she looked away, my Dad whispered in my ear saying, "You got this, just believe in yourself."

We sat down and she discussed what the University academic program had to offer. She also asked what I liked to be involved in. I told her that I loved fashion and retail management. I also like sports rehab as too. She went on to show me that the school didn't have those types of courses. She mentioned that they had a Business Marketing Degree Program. I wasn't in love with it, but it seemed to be ok to pursue. Heck in my mind, any degree would suffice. After a while of talking about academics and what the school had to offer for me, she discussed my current situation. She said, "I've heard what your father had to say about your grades from your current school. It's unfortunate that you have to go through this as a student-athlete. However, let me be frank. This is a private university and the course work is a lot tougher, but the classroom size is smaller. That will give you the advantage to build a one-on-one relationship with your professors. To further our discussion about recruitment, you must get your grades in order. Once you accomplish this then you're set." She looked at me in my eyes and said, "Your father is doing a wonderful job instilling values in you. I commend him for contacting me about your situation. Although he's doing what he should, from this moment on you must take control of your destiny. You can make it at this level if you're mentally prepared." I sat there and took every word in. I swallowed my pride and nodded my head, "Yes ma'am. I understand." She then stood up from her chair and took us on a small tour. She pointed to the direction where we would be going. We walked in front of her and my Dad looked over at me smiling. I smiled back. It was like we both were talking without having to say anything. I knew his smile meant, I'm here for you baby. And my smile meant Daddy, thank you so much. We made a sharp turn up the stairs to have a look at the gym. When I walked in, a few players were shooting around. The balls were almost patting on the court at the same time. Everyone had on the same colors, everything was in order and in sync. I walked passed them and they all were affixed, concentrating on their drills. They looked at me slightly but never strayed away from their task.

It was a short tour, but she went in detail as to what I needed to do for her to continue to consider me being a JU Dolphin. We all shook hands and we departed from one another. When we walked away, I sighed in relief. I said, "OMG! Daddy, How in the heck did you pull this off? I can't even breathe right now." He said to me like he always says, "She is your coach now, but I am your coach for life, remember that!" Soon as I thought things were over, we walked into the admissions office. I jokingly said, "So, Daddy where to next?" He said, "We have an appointment with someone in admissions. They will go in detail as to what you need for your acceptance."

Man, this was crazy! I'm sitting in the office twiddling my fingers waiting for them to call my name. Daddy rested his hands over mine and winked at me and said, "Nay chill! It's gonna be alright, trust me." Around the corner comes this tall woman. Ironically her name was Mrs. Davis. She greeted us with a warm welcome and we walked to her office. She asked us how our day was going and we both replied, "It's going great!" She complimented my Dad, telling me how wonderful he was. That there aren't too many parents that care so much about their child's success in this magnitude. She told me that I should be proud. I told her that I was. That I didn't have any idea about any of these meetings we had today. I expressed how shocked I was and questioned how was he able to do all of this on his own. She said, "When you're a parent, there will be things you'd have to do for your child. Things that may seem awkward to you now, but you won't understand what your father is doing until you become a parent yourself." I told her, "Yes, I'm not a parent and I truly don't understand that yet, but I am appreciative of everything that my parents do for me. I told her that I appreciated her as well, for taking the time out of her day to help assist me and leading me in the right direction."

We pressed on further and the conversation concluded with her telling me that to get approved, I must have a cumulative

3.0 GPA before the end of the summer. She told me with high regard that she believed in me. That she expects to see me walking the campus in the fall semester. She asked me if I was ready and I said, "Yes!"

🏀 Spring and Summer Grind 2004 🏀

When we left my dad said, "Alright I'm tired. I did my job here. Now you have to carry it on from here. You know what to do." He took me out to lunch and we went back home. In a few hours he had to go to work and so did I. All evening at my job, I pondered on everything that I needed to do. I wrote down my goals. I told myself; "Nay, Stay focused." I passed my spring classes. This time around I had tunnel vision. I didn't see anything on the side of me. I stood the course and moved forward with a PLAN. My summer schedule was moderate. I was the assistant store manager at my job and I had to be there to open at 9:45 am. I was no longer on scholarship, so I had to pay for my summer classes without my parent's help. I walked over to admissions at FCCJ and they gave me the total cost for my summer classes. They hit me over the head with the cost saying, "Miss Davis, The total amount for your summer classes comes up to $535.00." I held the print out they gave me in total shock. I said to myself, "Like, seriously?" The lady at the window answered saying, "Yes." When I walked away they said, "Oh and Miss Davis this doesn't include the cost of books, those are separate." (A Double Whammy!) I asked the person at the desk, "So I have to pay for my courses and my books separately?" She said with a blank stare, "Yes." I walked out of there mad. Completely agitated. How can this cost so much? I went home and told my parents and their reaction was, "Well, get to work my dear. Welcome to the real world." With heaviness on my soul, I walked in my room so flustered. My mother later explained to me that day saying, "This is what life is all about. You have highs and you have lows. You can't let the simple things get to you. You have to stay focused Jenarie."

I had a few weeks off before summer school started. This gave me time to work and save up to pay for my classes and books. My and class scheduled was tough. I had to complete two science courses and an English class. My English class started around 7:15 am to 9:30 am every Tuesday and Thursday. I explained this to my supervisor and mentioned that I will open the store at 10 am instead of 9:45 am due to my class schedule. He wasn't too happy about that, being that most of the stores in the mall would already be open by then. He asked me to do my best to be there. I couldn't promise him anything. Hey, he never fired me!

My science classes were Wednesday and Thursday if my memory serves me right. Those were evening classes. My work schedule was all over the place. I had to be there from 10 am to 10 pm. Taking an hour lunch and three 15 minute breaks. Or I'd work a split shift from 10 am to 3 pm reporting back to work from 5 pm - 10 pm. The weekends were even crazier. But I had to do what I needed to pay for my summer classes. That money also went towards my first semester at JU. Even though I didn't get accepted in at the time, I practiced speaking affirmations, telling myself that I will be a JU Dolphin in advance.

It was time to officially take my summer classes and boom. There I was back in the registrar office and paid for my summer classes and books with cash baby. I went to the bank and asked to make a withdrawal and I looked at all that money. Just sitting there on my lap. I was proud of myself. I worked hard for this money on my own. I didn't have to ask my parents for anything. I did it. I remember those days when I didn't have to open at work, I'd come to school early. I'd go to the second floor of the student commons building and watch Judge Mathis. This was my quiet time to concentrate and get ahead of the game. Even at work, I'd be multitasking. Studying and handling customers and doing inventory.

I was getting tired of studying and working all time. It seemed like it all would never end. But it did have an end. I checked my email and my final grades came in. I couldn't bare to open it. I needed a 3.0 cumulative GPA to get into JU. I opened my email and there it was. 3.0 on the dot! I rushed home so fast. I opened the house door and screamed out loud! "I got it! I did it! I got my 3.0!" My parents were really ecstatic.

They said, "We knew you could do it. Didn't we tell you that!" I was happy, but my job wasn't done yet. I had to pay for an application and an official transcript, before mailing it to JU.

So the wait began. I continued to go to work and resume my duties. Now mind you, I was still conditioning, (Keeping in shape). If I wanted to keep up with Division 1 players I had to condition myself. Everything was going in my favor. Until I got a phone call from JU Athletics. I rushed to answer it because I thought it was the coach calling to inform me that I made the team. Nope! That wasn't it. This phone call was to let me know that the Head Coach would be replaced by a new coach for the fall semester. I automatically felt let down, disappointed, saddened and heartbroken! I remember a few months prior to meeting with JU, there was a school that wanted me to play for them that offered me a full scholarship. It was a little further south and my parents thought it'll be best for me to stay closer to home. My first thought was, "Dang, I should have taken that offer. It wasn't a Division 1 school, but they would have paid for everything. Now I'm stuck! With the fall basketball season quickly approaching, I still wasn't signed. And on top of that, I had to wait to see if JU accepted me or not. It seemed like there was no hope for me. Every day I continued to go to work. I checked the mail and nothing. My face told my true feelings. My body language was sluggish and I was running off of smoke fumes. My mother saw how the wait was getting to me. She told me to stay steadfast and don't lose hope. It's coming.

One day I came home and didn't even bother to check the mail. When I settled in, I walked passed a pile of envelopes on the couch. I saw one that said Jacksonville University and grabbed it quickly. Before opening it, I stopped and prayed. Father Yah, please let this go well. I opened it and there it read. Congratulations! I ran around like a chicken with its head cut off. I yelled so loud screaming, "Mommy! I did it, I got in! Omg, I can't believe I got in. All that hard work paid off mommy." She told me, "I knew you could do it, baby."

 I'm An official JU Dolphin! 🏀

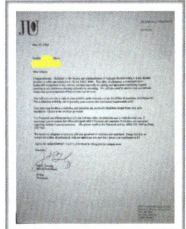 I was a little mad when I walked on campus. They had a welcome weekend event for incoming students and I was still salty about me not being signed as a women's basketball player. I kept telling my mother, who came along with me that I should be on the team. What does this mean for me now mommy? Maybe I shouldn't worry about playing ball! She said, "Stop and look at the good in what you were able to accomplish. You made it into one of the top private institutions in the South East Region. Forget about basketball for a minute. You put your brain to work for once and not your body. Be happy about that. Never mind basketball. If it comes it comes. The great thing is that you made it in. They can never take that away from you. Only you can defeat yourself. No one else!"

We walked the campus and I met a few people. It was totally different from what I was familiar with. All in all, I was excited. My workouts were going great. I felt like I was in great shape too. My work availability had to change a bit. I told my boss about it and he wasn't too happy. He relied on me to be present at work. Adapting to another school schedule wasn't in his plans.

My school work was coming along, but my job only got harder. My new goal was to find a way to meet with the new Women's Basketball Coach. "How could I impress her? What is she looking for in a player?" This was foreign to me. I was used to coaches knocking at my door, not the other way around.

One day I saw one of the players and asked her when will the coach be available. She was hesitant to tell me. She said, "She didn't know." She pointed to where her office was and I told her thank you and she walked off. I'm sure she thought I was weird to have asked her that. At the time it didn't phase me. I took a deep breath before walking into her office. It was the same office I walked into a few months prior and I was nervous all over again. Those same chills came over me. There was no time to freeze up now. So I walked in and it was cold in there. It was quiet too. I closed the door softly behind me and I said, "Hello. Is anyone here?" The coach faintly said, " Yes, please come in." She asked me if I needed help. I said, "Yes. I am a basketball player and would like to know if you were having tryouts for walk-on's this year." She looked at me and said, "Well, as of right now no we aren't. But if we do I'll be sure to inform you." In my mind, I was thinking how could she inform me if she doesn't even know who I am? I told her I played at FCCJ as a shooting guard. That I am capable of playing on the team. She nodded her head and said, "Thank you for sharing that with me. We will get back with you." I got it and told her, thanks for your time. And I walked out with my head between my legs. I felt so low. She didn't even consider anything I was saying. I told my mom and dad and they said, "You just have to keep calling her. Call her phone every day if you have to. Leave voicemails and emails too. Let her know how serious you are about playing." To me, in my opinion, I thought that was on some stalking type of vibes. I asked my mom, "Wouldn't you think she'd get tired of hearing from me if I did that." She said, "Yes Jenarie, that's the point. If she doesn't know who you are today, she'll know you in another week."

I pretty much did what my parents suggested. I called almost every day. Asking the coach if she was going to have tryouts for walk-ons and when? Sometimes she'd answer. Sometimes the other coaches would answer. I kept on being persistent. One day I got a phone call from the coach telling me when tryouts were. To be ready to play. I told my parents that she had called me back with a tryout date. They told me to keep in shape and to rest when I can to avoid me burning out.

🏀 The Night Before Tryouts 🏀

One night before tryouts, one of my friends asked if I wanted to play pick up with the guys to get a warm-up game in. I agreed and went with him. That evening we ran three pick-up games. The game was intense. Going back and forth with the score, it was our possession. As I was running back there was a loose ball that came on to our court and I tripped on it, rolling my ankle. It was hurt pretty badly, a sprain for sure. I grabbed it and yelled, "Dang Man! Come on! I have tryouts tomorrow, What am I going to do now?" The whole ride home I was wondering how my parents would feel about my injury.

My friend walked me inside the house. I couldn't bare to put any pressure on my foot. That's how much pain I was in. My mother saw me first. She said, "What in the world happened to you Jenarie?" I said, "I sprained my ankle." My dad just shook his head. My mom was mad the most though. She said," All that you worked for, is down the drain." I was so mad at myself. I should have just stayed home.

 What To Do Next? 🏀

My mom prayed over me that night. She said, "Rest your leg and drink plenty of fluids. You're going to those tryouts." I looked at her and said, "Mommy, How? Do you see my foot? Do you see how swollen it's gotten." She was adamant in what she said saying, "Like I said, you're going to those tryouts." My dad said, "You got into this, you're going to get yourself out of it." The day about an hour before tryouts, they helped me wrap my ankle. Bandaging it as tight as possible and I took like four extra strength Tylenol's and I got ready to leave. Before I left, my mom prayed over my ankle and said, "Do well tonight. I believe in you. We all do." I limped out of the house in so much pain. I drove to the tryouts barely able to press the gas. I ignored the pain and continued onward.

I walked into the gym from the back door. The coaches walked me and another walk-on candidate in the gym. There were about four players in the bleachers watching us. I felt like they were underestimating my talent. Hurt or not, they were in for a show. I was ready to prove myself. Have you ever felt pain so much that your soul began to itch? My pain level was way beyond 10. It was on 40. My ankle was throbbing so much

it felt like it wanted to pop right out of my shoe. All I could do is ignore the pain. My conscious was telling me, "If you want to be on the team, then you have to suck it up." I remember the line from the movie "A Long Kiss Goodnight," with Genna Davis and Samuel L. Jackson. Genna's name in the movie was Charlie. She told her daughter, who broke her arm that, "Life is pain, deal with it!" I closed my eyes and said a quick prayer. When I opened my eyes. I knew I was ready.

The coaches had us do drills and we played one-on-one to 5. We also had played two-on-two, which consisted of, Team #1 where one assistant coach and one walk-on player went against Team #2, one assistant coach and one walk-on player. With every step and every jolt, it felt as if my foot was tearing away from my bone. Even so, I kept praying to The Creator for strength. I keep asking that he hold me up and he did. I pushed through until the end.

Tryouts were over. I couldn't show how much pain I was truly feeling. The Tylenol was wearing off and I was ready to get in my car and go home. The head coach told us that they will call us to let us know if we made the team. They thanked us for coming and showed us out. When I was leaving, the scholarship players asked me for my name. I told them my name is Jenarie. They said, "J. You can ball girl." I thanked them and I walked up those stairs in agony. As soon as I got in the car I took my shoe off. My ankle was still wrapped and swollen.

I got out of the car and hopped on one leg all the way to the door. I put all my stuff down and hobbled in my parent's room. As soon as they saw me they both screamed! "Nay-Nay! You made it!" I said, Dang, y'all was waiting for me to come home that bad." In my mind I was like, Gosh I know I ain't dying. They said, "No crazy, you made the team. The coach just called." She said, "Tell Jenarie welcome to the team, she's a JU Dolphin!" Mommy and daddy hugged me so tight and we cried together. I'll never forget how I started. I'll always remember every sacrifice I had to endure to be successful.

Without my mother and father's guidance, I'd probably be somewhere living recklessly. I'm a product of someone never giving up on me. I am a product of love from a village of men and women. They shielded me and they reared me. The best thing they gave me was their time and their love. I finished college two years later, with a Minor in Marketing and Bachelors in Business Development and Leadership.

🏀 Final Thanks 🏀

I conclude by saying: Always put The Most High first. If you fail along the way, never give up. Learn from your failures. Teach those who come after you how to succeed. Teach them how to fail too. Let them know that they can accomplish anything that they put their minds to. Nothing can defeat you, but you. Keep pushing through, endure and stay focused. ~Jenarie

Rest in love to my Grandfather Leran, my godmother Mrs. Annette and my Great Grandparents James and Monda (Sarah) and Grandma Mildred. They were pivotal in my life. They gave me so much love and care. Sometimes their love required them to be stern and diligent. I didn't always enjoy their discipline. However, I knew it was needed. When we didn't have much, they were there to fill in the gaps. They were my solid foundation when I felt weak. Without their involvement, I'd have missing pieces to my already completed puzzle. They are definitely missed. Not just by me, but all of our families ache for them. They impacted the lives of so many others and that alone should say something. I will continue to speak about you and honor you, by sharing your essence with others who never knew you. I forever love you and appreciate you guys.

Love,

Your Nay

 **In Closing**

This book is for anyone who desires to learn how to play the game of basketball. The founders of Nike believe that everyone can be an athlete. Nike's mission states: *"Nike's mission is to bring inspiration and innovation to every athlete in the world. If you have a body, you are an athlete."*

Life experiences will teach you how to maneuver in society. Education improves your scope of thinking. Experience and education ties in together. They both go hand-in-hand. Our abilities and capabilities are based on how much effort we are willing to put into them. Complacency is a deterrent. Complacency is a hindrance. We ask ourselves if we are ready to put our capabilities to the test. Then when times present itself we have the opportunity to step beyond our comfort zones. We either complain about the task we have to complete or we wrestle with our cognitive and physical endurance. Can we endure the hardships that come with overcoming austerity?

 Life will make you lie down and call it Uncle. Are you deciding to give up on yourself when trouble comes, or are you prepared to conquer your goals no matter what? My story as a student-athlete invites you in to probe beneath the appealing surfaces. Success isn't fair or delightful as it may appear to be. You will have to prove that you are confident, skillful and adequate to cross that finish line. The beginning of any level is easy. Finishing, wrapping up the last stage of the journey you chose to embark on is proven to be the most difficult. Even so, when you pursue to reach every goal you set to attain, you will fall more than once, but you have to keep getting up. Our circumstances come with a two-edge sword. May it be good, bad or indifferent, we have to hold on to our principles and values.

Our support system (our village), provides our start in life. They give us the tools we need that are prerequisites to roadways we must follow. It's up to us to hold on to their teachings and apply them to our daily lives. It's our responsibility. We must further our potential. We're not only the gateway to the future, but we are the keys who unlock the entrance. Can you keep it open? Be a light to the children growing and learning behind you.

Their lives will hold The keys next. Leave clues for them to follow. They might stumble, but we have to trust them to become problem solvers. Life is a lesson and we all must learn.

We can't guarantee that you will love this book, but we ensure that it's a great read! One to have to share with everyone!
~Jenarie

Thank you for reading, "How To Play Basketball The Fun Way." I started this project sharing only vague details as how the sport of basketball should be played. Over the years, I found that the usefulness of the book will be well received if I included my testimony as a student athlete. I covered the basics and the most important aspects of what I experienced to give as an overview of the person that I once was. I wanted this book to relate to my readers. Every reader who is an aspiring beginner basketball player will learn how to incorporate exciting, enjoyable and playfulness within their fundamental techniques. All you have to do is have a positive attitude and be coachable. Learning comes from listening. Listen with a happy heart and then go out there and perform every step with joy. I believe in you.

Sincerely,

Jenarie (Ballers For L.I.F.E)